Puffin Books

Watch Out!
Keeping Safe Outdoors

It's not always easy to make yourself aware of the real
dangers which surround you outside the safety of your
own home and family. Here is a fun way for you to
learn about how to keep yourself safe.

Introduced by Fat Puffin and full of quizzes and
puzzles, readers can discover what to look out for:
where to play, how to cross the road and who it is safe
to talk to. There are sections on swimming, riding,
skateboarding and cycling, basic instructions on how to
use a phone box in an emergency, and what to do if
you get lost.

This is a fun, lively and comprehensive guide to safety
outside the home, written in co-operation with The
Royal Society for the Prevention of Accidents.

Rosie Leyden and Suzanne Ahwai have both worked
for the Health Education Council, writing and editing
health education material for the general public. They
are now co-partners in an editorial, print and design
service called *Wordworks* and live in London.

Produced in co-operation with
The Royal Society for the Prevention of Accidents

WATCH OUT!
Keeping Safe Outdoors

Rosie Leyden
and
Suzanne Ahwai

Illustrated by
Annie Horwood

and starring
FAT PUFFIN

Puffin Books

Acknowledgements

Grateful thanks to The Royal Society for the Prevention of Accidents for their advice on compiling this book, and for allowing us to use their *Play Wise Code* and material from *Be Water Wise*.

The authors would also like to thank Noreen Wetton, Consultant in Early Years Education at the University of Southampton, for her advice and helpful suggestions.

PUFFIN BOOKS

Published by the Penguin Group
Penguin Books Ltd, 27 Wrights Lane, London w8 5tz, England
Viking Penguin, a division of Penguin Books USA Inc.
375 Hudson Street, New York, New York 10014, USA
Penguin Books Australia Ltd, Ringwood, Victoria, Australia
Penguin Books Canada Ltd, 2801 John Street, Markham, Ontario, Canada l3r 1b4
Penguin Books (NZ) Ltd, 182–190 Wairau Road, Auckland 10, New Zealand

Penguin Books Ltd, Registered Offices: Harmondsworth, Middlesex, England

First published 1990
10 9 8 7 6 5 4 3 2 1

Filmset in Monophoto Baskerville
Printed in England by Clays Ltd, St Ives plc

Contents

Keeping Safe
Outdoors

What do you have to keep safe from outdoors?
Think about it.

Fat Puffin has some ideas about what he has
to keep safe from. Some of them are real
dangers, some are pretend ones. Which of these
are real? Which are pretend?

Answers on page 90.

Here are some things which **you** might have to keep safe from.

Which are real dangers?
Which are pretend ones?

Answers on page 90.

aliens

bullies

dares

gangs

ghosts

canals

crossing the road

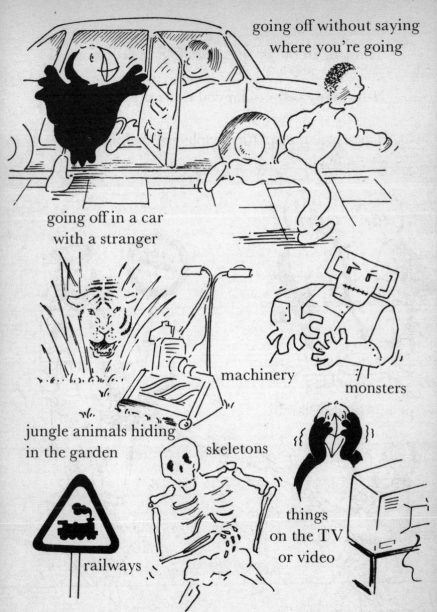

going off without saying where you're going

going off in a car with a stranger

machinery

monsters

jungle animals hiding in the garden

skeletons

railways

things on the TV or video

Before you turn over, think about this question:

Who keeps you safe from all these dangers?

Think of all the people who help to keep you safe.
How many people can you think of?

These are some of the people who help to keep you safe:

people in your family

fireman

school crossing
patrol warden

pool life-guard

policeman

your teacher

your friends

and
YOU

All these people help to keep you safe. But the most important person is **you**. This book is all about what **you** can do to keep safe outdoors.

How good are you at keeping yourself safe?
Try answering these questions:

1. How do you keep safe when you cross the road?
   a. I know the rules and keep to them.
   or
   b. I run across as quickly as I can.

2. How would you keep safe if someone dared you to do something silly?
   a. I would tell them that I don't do silly things.
   or
   b. I would try it, but I'd be very careful.

3. How do you keep safe when you are out
   with your mum or dad?
   a. I don't wander off on my own.
   or
   b. There's no need to worry because they
      watch me all the time.

4. How would you keep safe if a stranger talked
   to you?
   a. I would run away.
   or
   b. I would answer him or her politely.

Answers on page 90.

Be safety aware!

This book will help you to learn how to keep
yourself safe. It gives you lots of useful tips and
ideas. Look for this sign:

Monsters

Lots of people are afraid of pretend things like monsters or ghosts. Not just children, but grown-ups too. Sometimes these things seem very real.

Some people hide to keep away from danger. Or they run away. But usually the best thing is to talk to someone about it.

Safety TIP

If you ever feel frightened or if you don't feel safe, talk to someone you trust. Don't be afraid of looking silly.

Coming Out to Play?

Climbing, sliding, swinging, running . . .
Playgrounds are great fun.

CHILDREN'S
PLAYGROUND
Adults only admitted if
accompanied by a child

Play Wise Code

1. *Spot the dangers.*

You may think the playground is a safe place, but you can get hurt, especially when swinging, sliding and climbing. Learn to spot the dangers, avoid them and stay safe.

2. *Know the difference.*

There may be many different things for you to play on. Some are more difficult than others. Know what you can do safely and what is too difficult for you.

3. Check new places.

Each playground is different. Look around for any dangers that you have not seen before. Be especially careful when trying new apparatus for the first time.

4. Take safety advice.

There may be signs which are there to help you. Take notice of what they say. Listen carefully to any advice you may get from an adult – it will be for your own good.

DON'T STAND BEYOND THIS LINE

5. *Go with a grown-up.*

Parents like to play too. Take them with you. They can point out dangers and help you if you get into trouble. Never go to the playground alone!

6. *Learn how to help.*

You may be able to help yourself and others if you know what to do in an emergency. Know where the nearest telephone is so that you can ring for help if an accident happens. (See page 79 for how to phone for help.)

Don't try things that are
too difficult.

DON'T GO NEAR
THOSE MOVING
SWINGS, PUFFIN!

Listen to what your mum
or dad tells you.

What if someone dared you to do something like this?

I BET YOU CAN'T JUMP OFF THAT SWING.

1. *What would you think?*

– She'll think I'm a coward if I don't.
– I don't want to jump off because I might hurt myself.
– That's easy. Here goes.

Which answer is best?

2. *What could you say?*

– I don't do dares.
– Watch me. I'm going to jump.
– I'm not that stupid.

Which answer is best?

Answers on page 91.

Do you have a garden? If you do, imagine your friend is coming to play with you. What would you tell your friend about keeping safe in your garden?

Look at this picture. It might give you some ideas.

You'll find some ideas on page 91.

There are lots of signs that tell you if something is safe or dangerous. Learn how to recognize these signs:

Remember:

1. A sign in a red circle means 'Don't do . . .'

2. A sign in a red triangle warns people of a danger.

3. A blue circle with a white picture or white writing means 'You must do . . .'

Do you know what these signs mean?

Answers on pages 91–92.

Can you draw a sign to warn people about a dangerous place to play?

Places to play

Think about the places where you like to play.

Think of three safe places where you can play outdoors. Draw them or write them down.

Think of three safe places where you can play on your own. Draw them or write them down.

Show them to someone in your family or to your teacher. They will tell you if they think they are safe, and why.

Don't play

- on building sites
- on rubbish dumps
- near railways
- in empty houses

Going Places

How do you get to school?
How many roads do you have to cross?
Where is it most dangerous?
Can you draw a map or a picture of how you
go to school?
How do you keep yourself safe on your way to
school?

These ideas might help you.

Cross with the school crossing patrol warden.
Don't cross the road alone.
Cross with another family, or with someone
you know and trust, or with someone who
knows the Green Cross Code.

On the next page, Fat Puffin is using the Green
Cross Code.

The Green Cross Code

1.
First find a safe place to cross.

2.
Stop and wait near the kerb.

3.
Look all round and listen.

4.
If traffic is coming, let it pass.
Look all round again.

We've got to be patient.

At last!

5.
When there is no traffic near, walk straight across the road.

6.
Keep looking and listening.

Practise the Green Cross Code with grown-ups until you know how to cross the road safely.

31

A zebra crossing, pelican crossing or traffic lights are all safe places to cross the road. If you can't find one of these, try to find someone to help you cross. It might be someone in your family, or a person you know and trust.

This is a pelican crossing.

How to use a pelican crossing

The drawings show how to use a pelican crossing but someone has got them all mixed up. Can you put them in the right order?

1 If the red man shows, WAIT, even if there are no cars.

2 Then walk across quickly.

3 First you press the button.

4 Wait till the green man shows and bleeps.

Answer on page 92.

Safe places to cross the road

Can you find a safe way for Jo, Sam and Sharma to get to their school?

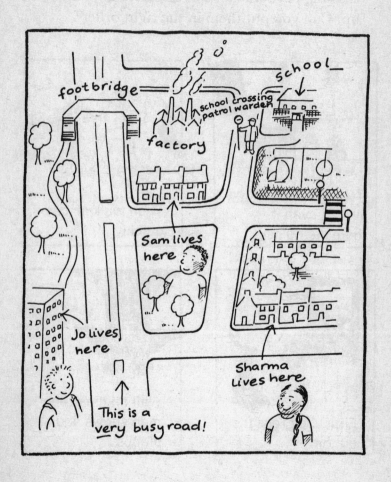

Answer on page 92.

Quiz

This is a safe person.   This is a safety silly.

Which of these things did the safe person say?

Which of these things did the safety silly say?

1. There are never many cars down our road, so there's no need to look before crossing.

2. It's best if you run across the road. Then you won't get knocked down.

3. I don't talk to my friends while I'm crossing the road.

4. I always try to cross the road at a zebra crossing or traffic lights.

Answers on page 93.

On narrow country roads, walk on the right-hand side of the road. Then you will be able to see any traffic coming towards you.

In winter, it gets dark early in the evening. It might even be dark when you come home from school.

It's a good idea to carry a torch. Also, it helps if you wear light-coloured clothes when you're out in the dark. Do you know why this is important? The experiment on the next page explains why.

Experiment

Get out some different-coloured clothes: socks,
jackets, coats and trousers. If you have any
reflective armbands, find them too. Put them
out at different points in your bedroom. Make
your bedroom as dark as possible, then shine
your torch quickly around the room.

Which clothes are the easiest to see in the dark?

Which are the most difficult to see?

At the station

Stay with your family or the grown-up you're with. If you do get lost, find a railway guard. He will help you find your family. He wears a uniform like this.

Keep away from the edge of the platform. And don't run around on the platform.

Wheelchair safety

If you use a wheelchair, or if you know someone who does, why not ask your teacher about the Wheelchair Proficiency Award Scheme?

You could get

– a Wheelchair Safety Certificate
– a Bronze Award
– a Silver Award
– a Gold Award

Your teacher can find out more about the scheme from:

Safety Education Department
The Royal Society for the Prevention of
   Accidents (RoSPA)
Cannon House
The Priory Queensway
Birmingham B4 6BS

Keeping Safe on Wheels

On your bike

Bikes can be great fun. You can go fast and feel the wind in your face.

Before you take your bike out on the road, you will need to get lots of practice.

Ask someone in your family to go with you.
They can give you some good tips.
Try to find a place where there's no traffic.
That's the best place to practise riding your
bike.

These are the things you can practise.

Getting on

Getting off

Starting

Stopping

Using the brakes

Riding along a line without wobbling

Looking behind without wobbling

Holding your hand out without wobbling

Cycling scheme

There is now a new cycling scheme called Cycleway which will help you become more aware while riding a bicycle. To find out more about Cycleway, contact:

Safety Education Department
The Royal Society for the Prevention of
    Accidents (RoSPA)
Cannon House
The Priory Queensway
Birmingham B4 6BS

Can you think of a keeping-safe message for children who ride bicycles?

BMX bikes

What makes accidents like this happen?

Can you think of some keeping-safe messages for children who ride BMX bikes?

What do they need to wear?
Where should they ride their bikes?
What do they need to practise?

Looking after your bike

If you have a bike, you will need to look after it so that it's safe to ride.

(You might need help from someone in your family.)

Check your bike for all these things.

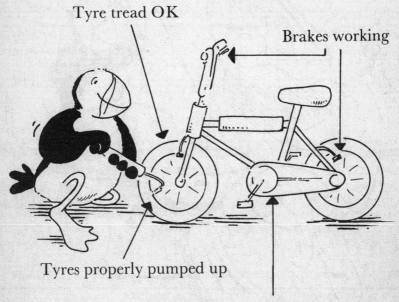

Tyre tread OK

Brakes working

Tyres properly pumped up

Chain properly adjusted and oiled

In the car

How can you help to keep yourself safe in the car?

Here are some ideas. Someone has got the words all mixed up. Can you put them right?

1. seat belt I my wear always.

2. driver bother the don't I.

3. my sisters argue don't brothers or I with.

Answers on page 93.

Look at these pictures of sportsmen and sportswomen. Can you tell what sport they are playing? Choose from the following:
horse-riding, skateboarding or rollerskating, American football, motorcycling.

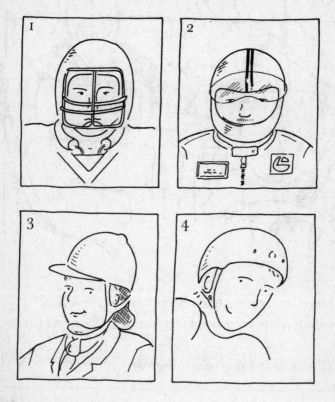

Answers on page 93.

Sportspeople think it is sensible to wear the right gear. It stops them from hurting themselves.

Skateboards and rollerskates

Look at this picture. Can you find two things which you could wear if you were skateboarding?

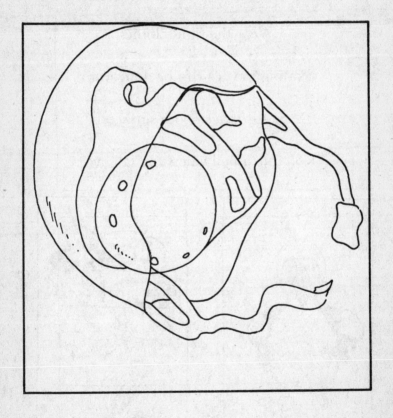

Answers on page 94.

Can you think of a keeping-safe message for someone who is rollerskating or skateboarding?

Rollerskating quiz

Can you match the pictures and the sentences?

Get your mum or dad to help you.

Wear the right clothes.

Skating too fast can be dangerous.

Skate on a smooth surface.

Roll into a ball when you fall over.

Answers on page 94.

In the Country

On a farm there are . . .
. . . places where it's fun and safe to play
. . . places where you should go only with
grown-ups you know and trust, and
. . . places where it's never safe to go.

On the farm

Look at these pictures. Which ones are of
places where it's **never** safe to go?

1.
A shed where
chemicals are
stored

2.
Where there are
high-voltage signs

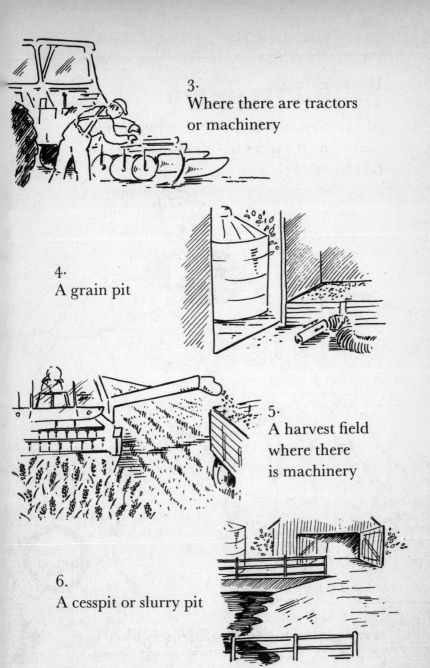

3.
Where there are tractors
or machinery

4.
A grain pit

5.
A harvest field
where there
is machinery

6.
A cesspit or slurry pit

Answers on page 94.

Horse-riding

Always wear the right sort of riding helmet. Make sure it carries the number BSI 4472 or BSI 6473.

Wear low-heeled, hard-soled shoes when you go riding.

Animals

Animals caring for their babies get very worried if another animal or a human goes near their babies. It's best not to go near animals when they are with their young.

Sows are especially dangerous, because they can attack someone who goes too near their piglets.

Safety TIP

Don't travel on the drawbar of a tractor.

Keep away from tractors and harvesters. These machines are very high and the driver may not be able to see you if you go too near.

Never play near ditches, streams or ponds.

Never climb on to a tractor or harvester or into a trailer unless the farmer tells you it's OK.

Near the Water

What do you do when you're at the swimming-pool?

Splash about? Swim? Paddle? Dive? Have races? Pretend to be a puffin? Play ball games? Have lots of fun?

It can be good fun swimming, but it can be dangerous too. So you need to learn how to keep yourself safe.

PARENTS, DID YOU KNOW?
Three-quarters of drownings happen inland in places like rivers, streams, lakes, reservoirs, canals and garden ponds. One quarter of drownings happen at the coast.

RoSPA produces a six-point code of advice which will help keep you safe, whether you are in the garden, by the river, at the seaside or at the swimming-pool. Here is how it will help you in two different places or locations.

Rivers, canals and streams

1. *Spot the dangers*

- The water may look harmless but there are often strong currents beneath the surface.
- Locks and weirs are dangerous places where the water is deep and powerful.

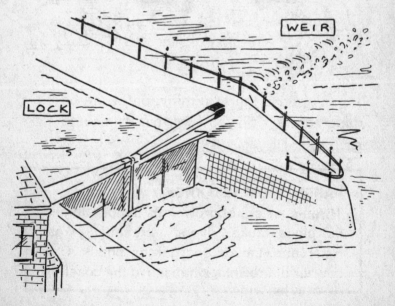

2. Know the difference

A swimming-pool is warm, clean, and supervised, whereas a river is none of these things. The currents of some rivers are too strong even for the best swimmers.

DANGER
Strong currents

3. Check new places

If you are visiting a place for the first time, make sure you know what the dangers are by asking someone.

4. *Take safety advice*

Take notice of any signs you might see.

5. *Be supervised*

Go only to rivers, canals and streams with an adult because they know what the dangers are and how to avoid them.

6. *Learn how to help*

Learn how to help yourself and others if an
accident happens. If you get into difficulties,
try to reach something to pull yourself to
safety. If you cannot, then get into a floating
position until help arrives. If someone else
gets into trouble, get an adult or use the
telephone to get help (see pages 79–80).

At the seaside

1. Spot the dangers

- The sea is different from other types of water because it has tides and currents which can sweep you away.
- Never use inflatable beds or toys on the sea because you could drift into deep water.

2. Know the difference

- It is far more difficult to swim in the sea than in the swimming-pool, because of the cold and tides.
- Make sure you swim parallel to the beach so that you do not swim out of your depth.

3. *Check new places*

New places may have hidden dangers that you do not know about. When you arrive at the seaside ask a policeman or another responsible adult to show you what the dangers are.

4. *Take safety advice*

Special flags and signs may warn you of danger. A red flag means do not enter the water. A red and yellow flag means that the beach is patrolled by life-guards.

5. *Be supervised*

- Always go to the beach with an adult.
- Only go into the water if your mum or dad or an adult tells you it is safe.

6. *Learn how to get help*

- If you get into difficulties, try to stay calm and call for help. Get into a floating position and wait for help to arrive.
- If you see someone else in trouble, either get the life-guard or use the telephone to get help (see pages 79–80).

Emergency!

What to do if you get into difficulty in the water.

1. Try to stay calm and call for help.

2. If the water is too deep for you to stand up, try to hold on to something: a rock or an overhanging branch.

3. If you can't hold on to anything, float on your back and wait for help.

If you see someone else in trouble at the seaside, call the life-guard and point to where the person is in distress.

Fire!

Why do people have fires outside? Here are some ideas:

To burn rubbish.
To celebrate Guy Fawkes night on November 5th.
To have a barbecue.

Can you think of any other reasons?

Here are some ways to keep safe when there is
a fire outside. Which do you think are good
ways?

Hide.
Keep away.
Don't try to help.
Never throw things on the fire.
Watch the little ones and the animals.
Tell a grown-up if you're scared.
Run indoors.
Answers on page 94.

Fireworks

November the 5th
Is Guy Fawkes night.
If you go near a bonfire
Your wings might catch light.

Can you unscramble these sentences?

1. fireworks throw never.

2. tin fireworks a the keep closed in.

3. put pocket never in your fireworks.

Answers on page 94.

Never try to light fireworks yourself. An adult
should light them for you.

Stand away from a lighted firework. Don't go
near it if it doesn't work straight away.

Out and About

When you are older, your mum or dad might let you go on short trips with your friends or on your own.

Who is in charge when you're out on your own? **You** are. So you have to know how to keep yourself safe. You have to know the rules and be able to keep them.

Safe people know their name.

Safe people remember their address.

Safe people remember their telephone number.

Safe people know how to get help if they get lost.

Would you know what to do if you got lost?
Look at the next page.

If you get lost . . .

Stay calm.

Look around to see if you can spot the people you were with.

Look for someone you can trust to ask for help.

If you're in a shop, you could ask a shop assistant.

If you're in the street, look for a policeman or policewoman, or a traffic warden.

If you're in a bus station or a railway station, look for someone wearing a uniform.

This is how to use a public telephone:

Learn how to use a telephone box.
These are some of the telephone boxes you
might see in the street.

If the box says 'Phonecard', you have to have
a special card before you can use the phone.
Otherwise you can use a coin.

1. Lift the receiver.

2. Put the coin in the slot.

3. Ring the number you want and wait for the person to answer.

Ask someone in your family to show you how to use a telephone box or to watch you do it.

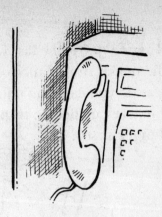

In an emergency

If you see an accident or a fire, someone must
phone for help. If there is no grown-up who
can do this, you might have to do it yourself.
Would you know what to do?

1. Find a telephone.

2. Lift the receiver and ring 999. You don't
   have to put any money in.

3. You will hear a voice asking:
   'Which service do you want?'

   Ask for
   'Police' or
   'Ambulance' or
   'Fire brigade'.

   They will put you through straight away to the
   right people.

Ringing 999 is the fast way to get help from the police, ambulance or fire brigade. At the seaside you can ring 999 to get the coastguards. They rescue people trapped on cliffs or in danger at sea.

Don't phone 999 unless you really need to. But nobody will mind if you ring 999 when you're not sure what to do, or if you are frightened.

People who scare you

Who are the people you're scared of?

What can you do to keep safe from the people who scare you? Here are some ideas. Which do you think are the best ideas? Can you think of some more?

Stay away from them.

Stay with your friends.

Run away.

Tell an adult that you're scared. (Remember that lots of grown-ups are scared of things too.)

How can you tell if someone might want to hurt you? The answer is that you can't tell.

Most people are good and kind. But some people are not. You can't tell who is good and who is bad just by looking at them.

If a stranger talks to you:

– Don't answer.
– Don't try to help him or her.
– Never take anything from him or her.
– Never walk with the stranger or get into his or her car.
– Tell your parent or a teacher or a policeman as soon as you can.

Safety TIP

Secrets

Fat Puffin has got a good secret. Fat Puffin isn't telling anyone.

Do you ever have good secrets you share with people? Do you tell?

Just sometimes, people might try to make you keep a bad secret. They might say you'll get into trouble if you tell.

This is the time to tell. Find a person you trust and tell them.

1. How would you keep yourself safe . . .

. . . on the footpath or pavement?
. . . at the swimming-pool?
. . . crossing the road?
. . . on your bicycle?
. . . on the beach?
. . . by the river or canal?
. . . in a crowd?
. . . near the railway track?
. . . if you go out on your own?
. . . if you're out with your friends?

Here are some ideas to help you. You can use as many ideas as you like for each question.

I can say no.
I know the rules.
I keep calm.
I keep away.
I don't show off.
I think for myself.
I don't do dares.
I keep to the rules.
I look and listen.
I know who is in charge.
I don't play about.
I say where I'm going.
I don't let people push me about.

2. What would you do . . .

. . . if you were with your friend and your
friend ran across a busy road?

. . . if you saw a friend going off in a car with
a stranger?

. . . if your friends were doing wheelies on their
bikes down the main road and they dared
you to try it?

3. How would you keep safe from . . .

. . . people you don't know who ask you to go
off with them?

. . . people who want you to do stupid,
dangerous things?

. . . frightening things you see on TV?

. . . pretend things like ghosts, monsters, witches
and gremlins?

There are lots of possible answers to this quiz. The answers depend on how old you are and how much you know about keeping yourself safe. The best thing is to talk about your answers with someone in your family, or with your teacher.

Poster Contest

Can you help Fat Puffin choose the best safety poster? Which one is your favourite?

Answers

pages 8–9

The real dangers for Fat Puffin are:
1. crossing the road
4. broken glass on a beach

The pretend dangers are:
2. the ghost
3. the monster

pages 10–11

The pretend dangers are:
aliens
ghosts
jungle animals hiding in the garden
monsters
skeletons
things on the TV or video

All the others are real dangers.

pages 14–15

1a; 2a; 3a; 4a.

page 23

1. 'I don't want to jump off because I might hurt myself.'

2. 'I don't do dares' or
   'I'm not that stupid'.

pages 24–5

What you could tell your friend depends on what is in your garden, but here are some ideas:
Never go near the lawn mower.
Never play near the pond.
Keep the garden gate shut.
Never eat any berries or plants.
Never touch any chemicals that your family keeps in the garden shed.
Never go near a bonfire.

pages 26–7

1. This is a school crossing patrol warden's sign. It warns drivers to stop because there are children crossing the road.

2. Keep away. There are high-voltage electricity lines near here.

3. Beware of falling rocks.

4. Beware of the dog.

5. Keep out of this derelict house. It's dangerous.

6. Keep away from the water here. You may fall in.

page 33

The correct order is:
3, 1, 4, 2

First you press the button.
If the red man shows, WAIT, even if there are no
  cars.
Wait till the green man shows and bleeps.
Then walk across quickly.

page 34

Jo crosses by the footbridge and then with the school
crossing patrol warden.

Sam crosses with the school crossing patrol warden.

Sharma crosses on the zebra crossing.

page 35

The safe person said 3 and 4.
The safety silly said 1 and 2.

1. Even if there are not usually many cars on the road, one might come just as you are about to cross.

2. If you run across the road, you might fall over. It's best to walk across quickly.

3. If you talk to your friends while you're crossing the road, you might forget to look out for traffic coming.

4. Zebra crossings or traffic lights are safe places to cross the road. Other safe places are: footbridges, subways, pelican crossings, or where there is a school crossing patrol warden to help you.

page 49

1. I always wear my seat belt.
2. I don't bother the driver.
3. I don't argue with my brothers or sisters.

page 50

1. American football
2. motorcycling
3. horse-riding
4. skateboarding or rollerskating

page 51

The two things hidden in the picture are:
a knee pad
a helmet

pages 52–3

1. Wear the right clothes.
2. Skate on a smooth surface.
3. Get your mum or dad to help you.
4. Skating too fast can be dangerous.
5. Roll into a ball when you fall over.

pages 54–5

It's never safe to go to **any** of the places in pictures 1–6.

page 69

Ways to keep safe are:
Keep away.
Never throw things on the fire.
Watch the little ones and the animals.
Tell a grown-up if you're scared.

page 70

1. Never throw fireworks.
2. Keep the fireworks in a closed tin.
3. Never put fireworks in your pocket.

Index